Penny Whiting's guide

— THE —
AMERICA'S CUP

REED

® & © America's Cup Properties Inc.

Established in 1907, Reed Publishing (NZ) Ltd
is New Zealand's largest book publisher, with over 300 titles in print.

For details on all these books visit our website:
www.reed.co.nz

Published by Reed Books, a division of Reed Publishing (NZ) Ltd,
39 Rawene Rd, Birkenhead, Auckland 10.
Associated companies, branches and representatives throughout the world.

ISBN 0 7900 0848 3
First published 2002

Edited by Carolyn Lagahetau
Designed by Graeme Leather
Cover designed by Craig Violich
Cover photograph by Ivor Wilkins

Printed in New Zealand

Contents

Foreword

It's been fun gathering facts about America's Cup sailing into one small book. My intention has been to give you an idea of what those sailors are doing out there (I know they just seem to be going around in circles!).

I am constantly asked questions about the tactics and manoeuvres involved with sailing in the America's Cup or Louis Vuitton Cup races. In this book I've tried to provide the answers to the most frequently asked questions, doing so in a format and in language that is easy to read and understand. Some of the questions I get asked are, 'Why are the boats going in different directions?', 'What's a layline?', 'Why are there only two boats in each race?' and 'How many crew are on a boat and what *are* they doing?'

With the determined assistance of researcher Elisa Duder, we have put the facts together for you, hopefully so that you can understand and enjoy the sailing both on the water and in front of the television.

My editor at Reed Books, Carolyn Lagahetau, is not a sailor and has been wonderful at asking me the questions you all want the answers to. Carolyn has been committed to helping me make this book make sense for you.

Several members of Team New Zealand and Dean Salthouse have been checking on the rules and facts I have written about, making sure I am on the correct tack.

Line 7 and Ross Munro and his team continue to support me with suitable sailing clothes; I really appreciate their contribution.

Many thanks to my friend and America's Cup veteran, Rob Maw, whose experience in sailing these boats has been invaluable.

My son Carl, as one of the Team New Zealand sailors, has made valuable comments about sailing these amazing yachts and I value his input. He constantly reminds me that an America's Cup yacht is a very expensive and highly tuned piece of equipment — quite different to your everyday sailing yacht.

My daughter Erin has often said, 'Come on, Pen, let's work out which yacht is going to get to the mark first!', and her enthusiasm for the sailing also keeps me focused on helping you understand and enjoy seeing the thrill of America's Cup yacht racing.

I love sailing and mucking about in boats — I hope this book helps you understand why so many of us love to sail and float about in yachts as much as we do.

What is the
America's Cup?

The America's Cup regatta is a match-racing series held approximately every three to four years between two teams, a **Defender** and a **Challenger**. The Defender is the winner of the previous America's Cup and the Challenger is the winner of the Louis Vuitton Cup, which is held just before the America's Cup.

In 2000 the Defender was Team New Zealand because they had won the America's Cup in San Diego in 1995, against *Young America*. Team New Zealand is the Defender in 2003.

Teams race to be trustees of the silver trophy known as the America's Cup, now at the Royal New Zealand Yacht Squadron. The Royal New Zealand Yacht Squadron is the host of the 2003 regatta.

> The Cup itself was made by Garrard & Sons in London.
>
> The 'Auld Mug' is a bottomless, silver ewer.
>
> It weighs in at 134 ounces (about 3.8 kilograms)
> and stands about 27 inches (68 centimetres) high.

Match racing

Match races are races between two boats of the same class. There can be more than two boats racing in a match race, but in the America's Cup only two boats race at a time. In fleet racing it is possible to have large numbers of boats that are quite different in design that rely on a handicapping system to even out the competition.

Both the Louis Vuitton Cup and the America's Cup are held under match-racing rules set out by the International Sailing Federation.

The Louis Vuitton Cup

The Louis Vuitton Cup is awarded to the winner of the Challenger or Elimination Series that is held before the America's Cup regatta. In 2000 the winner was the Italian syndicate Prada, in *Luna Rossa*. Prada became the Challenger against Team New Zealand.

In 2003 there are nine international syndicates competing for the Louis Vuitton Cup. There are teams from France, Great Britain, Italy, Sweden, Switzerland and the United States of America. Italy has two teams and there are three teams from the United States of America.

Louis Vuitton, a Paris-based luggage maker, became

the sponsor of the Challenger Series in 1983.

The first winner of the Louis Vuitton Cup

was *Australia II.*

What is a syndicate?

A syndicate is made up of anything between 60 and 130 people. The group includes designers, sailmakers, the weather team, shore crew, the sailing team and the group of people who handle the business side of running a syndicate.

Today, there are huge corporations spending upward of US$70 million to race for the America's Cup. Historically, syndicates have been funded by a few wealthy yacht club members, trials for the Cup would begin as little as four months before the actual Cup regatta, and the yachts would be sailed by amateur sailors.

Today's teams are fully paid employees. They stay together for the entire period of three or four years between Cup regattas. Being a member of a Cup team is a full-time job and career for those involved.

The lead-up from one Cup regatta to the next actually begins before the present regatta is completed. Long-range planning is a given within America's Cup challenges and defences and this includes keeping the majority of the syndicate team intact.

Boat design

One of the most important aspects of syndicate work is the boat design, which is an ongoing process. The introduction of the America's Cup-class yachts in 1995 showcased yachts that were suited for the conditions around the San Diego area — Pacific Ocean swells, which are quite large and often far apart and average winds of 5 to 12 knots but rarely more than 18 knots.

For the 2000 America's Cup, the yachts had to be designed for New Zealand conditions — no ocean swells, flatter water, short chops and winds between 5 and 25 knots. **Hull, keel** and **rudder** designs were altered to suit New Zealand conditions, as were sail shapes.

The design process is as important as any other aspect of an America's Cup campaign. A lot of time and effort goes into this process, along with a lot of secrecy!

Over the last 20 years the design process has changed from being the work of one designer or firm from outside the syndicate who was responsible for hull, deck layout, keel and rudder design, a **mast** builder who would build the mast to fit the yacht, and a sailmaker who would design and build the sails. There was little communication between the three groups, therefore there was little co-ordination between these stages of construction and little idea of how it would all fit together.

Today, syndicate design teams are inclusive of all factions of the yacht's construction. They work in close conjunction with each other at every step of the way.

Boat materials

Materials for boat construction have changed from wood to aluminium to fibreglass to Kevlar, and now to carbon fibre. The same process has happened to sail materials: firstly constructed of cotton, then nylon and Dacron to Mylar with Kevlar and carbon fibre-moulded sails. Yacht materials have developed into a very high-tech industry that uses space-age materials and techniques.

Testing the boats

Tank testing to find the fastest hull, keel and rudder shapes is ongoing. These facets of the boat are then put together with the best-suited **rig**, mast and sails. New Zealand's Tom Schnackenberg tested sails in wind tunnels during the 1995 campaign in San Diego. He eventually added all the elements together — the shape of the hull, keel, rudder, mast and sails — and came up with an unbeatable combination.

Why do the teams have two boats?

Using two boats from a previous campaign and all the information gathered about these boats, a syndicate will build two new boats. These are usually of new design using information gained from on-the-water sailing and tank and wind-tunnel testing.

The defending team has an advantage in that it usually does not have to compete in an elimination series, so it can reveal its yacht design later than the challengers.

The yachts can be designed for a smaller window of weather. The Louis Vuitton Cup races are sailed from October until January, usually in stronger winds than in February, when the America's Cup races are held. However, this can sometimes backfire if unusual weather occurs.

Two yachts allow the crew and the designers to test a variety of combinations of crew, sails and design innovations.

New Zealand syndicate success

The design process plays a major part in America's Cup competition. In recent regattas this became most obvious when New Zealand won in San Diego under the leadership of Sir Peter Blake and Tom Schnackenberg. Blake and Schnackenberg proved to be the most successful syndicate at putting the different elements of design together. They paid special attention to the engineering and manufacturing of all the moving bits and pieces on their yacht, the result being far fewer breakages on board compared to other yachts in the competition. The crew were consulted about deck layout, each person having input about the area on the boat in which they work and saying how they thought it could be better designed. In hindsight, it can be said that while the crew sailed brilliantly, the series was basically won before the boat left the dock as it was so meticulously prepared and designed.

As a result of New Zealand's approach to the design and syndicate process, the other 2000 and 2003 America's Cup syndicates have followed their lead in an effort to emulate their success.

The teams for
2003

The Defender

Previous America's Cup races have had a Defender Series, held when more than one syndicate from the defending yacht club has wanted to be the Defender. Team New Zealand is the only Defender representing New Zealand in 2003.

> **Yacht club**
> Royal New Zealand Yacht Squadron
>
> **Syndicate name**
> Team New Zealand
>
> **Syndicate heads**
> Tom Schnackenberg, Ross Blackman, Dean Barker
>
> **Sail number**
> NZL 81

The Challengers

To date, there are nine teams representing six countries registered to challenge the America's Cup in 2003. The first yacht club to register was the New York Yacht Club and they negotiated the rules with the RNZYS on behalf of the other challengers. The number of teams competing in the Louis Vuitton Cup may change leading up to the cup; some syndicates, although they have been assigned sail numbers, may not use them.

The following information is as up-to-date as possible at the time of publication of this book. There are some gaps for you to fill in as information becomes available leading up to and during the time of racing.

France

YACHT CLUB AND SYNDICATE NAME   Union Nationale pour la Course au Large

SYNDICATE HEAD/S

SAIL NUMBER/S   FRA-69

YACHT NAME

Great Britain

YACHT CLUB AND SYNDICATE NAME   Royal Ocean Racing Club

SYNDICATE HEAD/S

SAIL NUMBER   GBR-70

YACHT NAME   *Wight Lightning*

Italy

YACHT CLUB AND SYNDICATE NAME   Yacht Club Punta Ala Syndicate

SYNDICATE HEAD/S

SAIL NUMBER   ITA-74

YACHT NAME

Italy

YACHT CLUB AND SYNDICATE NAME   Reale Yacht Club Canottieri Savoia
    SYNDICATE HEAD/S
       SAIL NUMBER   ITA-72
          YACHT NAME

Sweden

YACHT CLUB AND SYNDICATE NAME   Gamla Stans Yacht Sallskap
    SYNDICATE HEAD/S
       SAIL NUMBER   SWE-63
          YACHT NAME

Sweden

YACHT CLUB AND SYNDICATE NAME   Gamla Stans Yacht Sallskap
    SYNDICATE HEAD/S
       SAIL NUMBER   SWE-73
          YACHT NAME

Switzerland

YACHT CLUB AND SYNDICATE NAME   Société Nautique de Genève/Alingi
    SYNDICATE HEAD/S
       SAIL NUMBER   SUI-64
          YACHT NAME

Switzerland

YACHT CLUB AND SYNDICATE NAME   Société Nautique de Genève/Alingi
    SYNDICATE HEAD/S
       SAIL NUMBER   SUI-75
          YACHT NAME

USA

YACHT CLUB AND SYNDICATE NAME   Seattle Yacht Club/One World
    SYNDICATE HEAD/S
       SAIL NUMBER   USA-65
          YACHT NAME

USA

YACHT CLUB AND SYNDICATE NAME   Seattle Yacht Club/One World
   SYNDICATE HEAD/S
      SAIL NUMBER   USA-67
         YACHT NAME

USA

YACHT CLUB AND SYNDICATE NAME   Golden Gate Yacht Club/Oracle
   SYNDICATE HEAD/S
      SAIL NUMBER   USA-71
         YACHT NAME

USA

YACHT CLUB AND SYNDICATE NAME   Golden Gate Yacht Club/Oracle
   SYNDICATE HEAD/S
      SAIL NUMBER   USA-72
         YACHT NAME

USA

YACHT CLUB AND SYNDICATE NAME   New York Yacht Club/Dennis Conner
                                Stars & Stripes
   SYNDICATE HEAD/S
      SAIL NUMBER   USA-66
         YACHT NAME

USA

YACHT CLUB AND SYNDICATE NAME   New York Yacht Club/Dennis Conner
                                Stars and Stripes
   SYNDICATE HEAD/S
      SAIL NUMBER   USA-77
         YACHT NAME

Who makes **the rules?**

Deed of Gift

The Deed of Gift was presented to the New York Yacht Club with the silver cup in 1887. The Deed is the base rules document for the America's Cup and has been modified throughout America's Cup history by Trustee Interpretive Resolutions. It also allows for other rules and conditions to be agreed, by mutual consent, between the Defender and the Challenger.

In recent events these rules have been incorporated in a document known as The Protocol. The Protocol is agreed before each America's Cup between the defending yacht club and the first yacht club to issue the challenge.

If a Protocol is not agreed the parties revert to the provision of the Deed of Gift that occurred in the 1988 Big Boat versus Catamaran event.

The Protocol

The Protocol becomes the governing document for the current America's Cup. It has been negotiated between the yacht club defending the Cup, the Royal New Zealand Yacht Squadron, and the Challenger of Record, which is the first yacht club to register a challenge. For the 2003 America's Cup, the Challenger of Record is Yacht Club Punta Ala.

The Protocol outlines how the Louis Vuitton Cup and America's Cup regattas are to be run. Each syndicate is allowed two yachts and a set of 60 sails.

The Protocol has also established an America's Cup Arbitration Panel to hear and rule on disputes between defenders and challengers. This was established to avoid disputes over the Deed of Gift going to the courts.

Finally, there are the *racing rules.* This are set out by the International Yacht Racing Federation for Match Racing. They specify how races are organised, run and raced.

International
Match Racing Rules

The rules for racing are set out in the Notice of Race and Conditions issued by the present trustee of the Cup.

The International Sailing Federation issues the *International Match Racing Rules*. The America's Cup regatta may have modifications made to some rules, but these modifications have to be agreed to by both the Defender and the Challenger of Record for each regatta.

Umpires

Since 1992, on-the-water umpires have been used to see that the teams adhere to the rules. The umpires follow the yachts in chase boats. The aim of on-the-water-umpires is to avoid lengthy protests after the race.

In close-quarter situations, one of the yachts will always have **right of way**. The two umpires behind the respective yachts are constantly talking to each other to see if a yacht is in breach of the rules.

Penalties

Any violation of the rules is penalised on the water by the on-the-water umpires, as the race is being run. A penalty may require a yacht to perform a penalty turn (which is a circle from its present course). Whether the penalty is performed immediately or at another time during the race is indicated by the flags used by the umpires.

Protests

If there are any technical protests and disputes that are not dealt with by the on-the-water umpires and require a ruling after a race, each team is heard by an international jury that conducts a hearing. The jury can rule for disqualification if a team is found to have violated the rules.

Strategy

A basic knowledge of the match-racing rules and terminology is helpful when watching the racing on television, because commentators use these rules to interpret what the boats are doing and why.

Yacht-racing strategy is a combination of an intimate knowledge of the rules, knowing how the boat works, the conditions and environment in which sailing is taking place, and an ability to anticipate where a rival is going to be and often trying to block his moves!

The
races

The Challenger Series
culminating in the Louis Vuitton Cup

Syndicates from around the world register with the Defender to be a
Challenger and to race in the Challenger or Elimination Series run before
the America's Cup regatta. This series will run between October 2002 and
January 2003. The teams race each other in a series of **round robins**.

In round robins 1 and 2 each team races all the other teams,
gaining 1 point for each win.

Round robin 3 is raced between the top eight teams.
These eight boats are split into two groups.

The first four boats from the previous round robins are in the Double
Chance Group and with the way the quarterfinals are structured they only
have to race once more to be in the Final Round Robin. This is to give the
stronger teams more preparation time for the final races of the Louis
Vuitton Cup, instead of continuing to race against other syndicates.

The second group, the Single Chance Group, is made up of the last four teams to be in the quarterfinals. This group has to race two more races than the first group to be able to be in the Louis Vuitton Cup final. The team sailing the best of seven races wins.

Round Robin 1	Each team races against all the other teams and receives 1 point per win.	15 boats
Round Robin 2	Each team races against all the other teams and receives 1 point per win.	15 boats

The top 8 boats go through to Quarterfinals 1

	SINGLE CHANCE GROUP	DOUBLE CHANCE GROUP	
Quarterfinals 1 *Best of 7 races*	▲ ❖ ✳ ■	● ★ ✖ ◆	8 boats
Quarterfinals 2 *Best of 7 races*		◆ ★ ✖ ●	4 boats
Semifinals 1 *Best of 7 races*	❖ ✳	● ★	4 boats
Semifinals 2 *Best of 7 races*		❖ ★	2 boats
Finals LOUIS VUITTON CUP *Best of 7 races*	✳ ★		2 boats
Challenger	✳		1 boat

22

A typical race day

After an early morning gym session, the crew arrives at the compound at around 7 a.m. The following schedule could differ on race days.

The crew get the two boats ready to launch (boats are always hauled out of the water after every sail to prevent marine growth adhering to the hull).

The **afterguard** (and sometimes the trimmers) consult with the weather team and plans are made on the expected forecast.

Each team meets and talks about the day.

Boats are launched and decisions are made about what sails go on the race yachts and what sails will go on the chase boat.

Both boats leave the Viaduct Harbour under tow quite slowly. When they get out into the harbour they are towed quite fast (around 10 knots). If you plan to go out to the course with them you need to be able to go fast to keep up!

Once near the course, the competing boats put the sails on and start sailing together to check speeds and decide how they are going to handle the conditions of the day. At this point there is lot of communication with the weather team, who are strategically placed around the course.

As starting time nears, decisions must be made as to what sails need to be on the boat for the race and what sails will stay on the chase boat. The two boats sail **upwind** and **downwind** to check their speeds against each other. Seaweed and other debris can get caught on the keel **wings** or rudder; by sailing together they are able to check these things.

An America's Cup yacht has only one **mainsail** aboard for each race, along with **spinnakers**, **gennakers** and **genoas**.

Sail selection is often done just before preparation for the start line.

No further communication with weather teams is allowed after the starting sequence has commenced.

Spectator boats have a defined area to watch from and they must keep well clear of the starting box and its surrounding area. This area is marked off with buoys and small boats.

Sometimes the race can be delayed or postponed due to the wind direction changing and/or too little or too much wind. The chase boats and the extra sails are never far away. Sometimes during a race a yacht will have to change to a different size of genoa if there is a significant change in wind strength on the upwind leg of the race. This is done by sliding one sail up a twin track on the forestay, while the other sail is still being used to sail the yacht. With fantastic crew work the other sail comes down and they are sailing with a different combination of sails because the conditions are different.

In Auckland there is up to a 3-metre tide change every six hours. The wind direction and sea conditions can change at the same time, causing havoc on the race course when the top mark is not directly to **windward** of the committee boat (which indicates one end of the start line). Sometimes the races are stopped and the course is reset, so the whole starting procedure begins again.

Rules of
interest

There are some basic rules that determine which boat has the right of way. However closely the skipper and tacticians sail to the rules, they are always expected to leave the other yacht an avenue of escape and to take steps to avoid collision, even if they have right of way.

Right of way

There are two basic rules (these also apply to sailing in general, not just to match racing).

Port and starboard rule

1 Boats on **starboard** tack have right of way over boats on **port** tack. This means the wind is hitting them on the right side of the boat or both sails are on the left side.

Windward keeps clear of leeward

2 If the yachts are on the same tack with the wind on the same side, the **windward** boat is closer to where the wind is coming from and has to keep clear of the boat to **leeward** (where the wind is going). So, the leeward boat may push up the windward boat by **heading** them into the wind and forcing them to tack.

Overlap

An important aspect that applies in many situations determining right of way is **overlap**. This occurs when the following boat's **bow** (front) crosses the straight line from the lead boat's **stern** (back).

Crew members on the stern or bow of the boat indicate overlap by waving an outstretched arm up and down. In the diagram, the left-hand boat would normally give way to the boat on the right because they are to windward. However, because the following boat has overlapped the perpendicular line off the stern of the left-hand boat, it now has to keep clear.

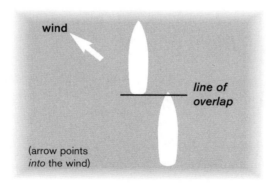

Overlap is important when the yachts are going round the marks. If the yachts are on a downwind run, the following yacht might get an inside overlap (more than two boat lengths from the mark), which allows it to round first and be in a controlling position to start the upwind leg. The rules take into account which team created the overlap.

Why is the
yacht sailing
that way?!

It is helpful to know some basic rules
of sailing when watching yacht racing.

1 No yacht can sail directly into the wind.
The nearest angle a yacht can sail to the wind
is 30° from the side the wind is coming from.

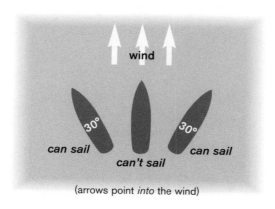

wind

30°

30°

can sail

can't sail

can sail

(arrows point *into* the wind)

2 If a yacht wants to get to where the wind is coming from it will tack from one side of the wind to the other. The tide, different strengths of wind at different angles and tactical positions with regard to the other boat govern when a boat will tack.

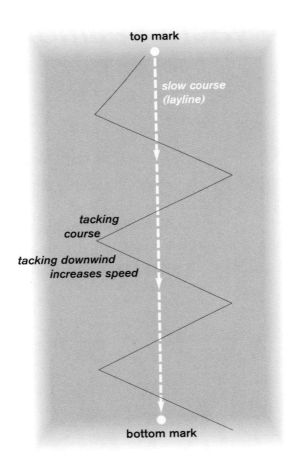

top mark

slow course
(layline)

tacking
course

tacking downwind
increases speed

bottom mark

Tacking is changing direction by **going about** or **gybing**. Sailing upwind is also called **on the wind, beating, bashing, slogging** or **close-hauled**. These days on the wind is also called a *dead maggot*!

A yacht is on either port tack or starboard tack, depending on which side the wind hits the yacht. If the wind is coming from the *port (left) side* of the yacht, it is on the *port tack*. If the wind hits the *starboard (right) side* of the yacht, the boat is on the *starboard tack*. If the wind directly hits the back of the yacht and the main **boom** is to port (left), the yacht is on a starboard tack. If the wind directly hits the back of the yacht and the main boom is to starboard (right), the yacht is on port tack.

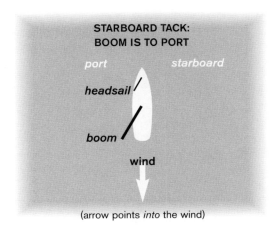

(arrow points *into* the wind)

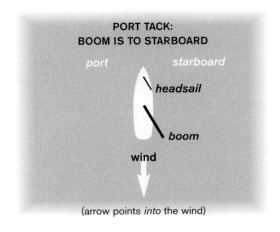

(arrow points *into* the wind)

America's Cup yachts sail with a mainsail and a headsail (also called a genoa) and a spinnaker or gennaka. The sails are shaped like an aeroplane wing so that they give lift as well as forward movement. Both sails give these yachts power. The slot between the two sails is also very important to help the yacht sail closer to the wind and the top mark of the course. Crew are constantly reshaping the sails to look like aeroplane wings as these provide the yacht's speed and power.

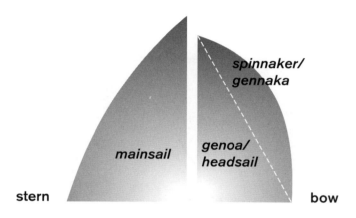

spinnaker/ gennaka

mainsail

genoa/ headsail

stern

bow

The further **forward** the wind hits a yacht the further *in* the sails have to be. As the wind moves aft to the stern of the boat the sails go out until the wind is behind the boat. At this point the sails are all the way out.

When the wind hits a boat on the **beam** (the middle of the boat) the sails should be halfway out.

In the America's Cup course, the yachts travel upwind or downwind. They often use wide angles going downwind for extra speed, at the same time covering more distance than if they took a straight course to the next mark.

The less the rudder is turned, the better. Good sail **trim** stops the helmsman from having to turn the **wheel** (which is attached to the rudder) a lot, as the wheel acts like a brake in a car if it is turned too much.

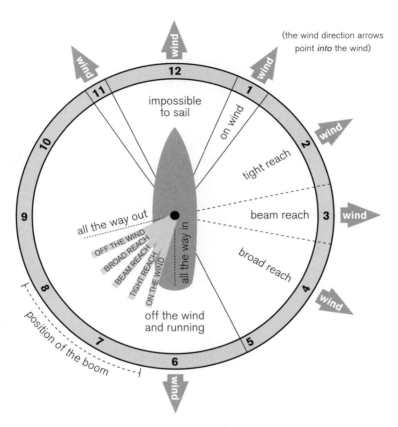

(the wind direction arrows point *into* the wind)

Points of sailing
the different angles to the wind on which a boat may sail

off the wind to sail downwind.

broad reach with the wind aft, any point of sailing between a beam reach and running.

beam reach wind hitting on the beam.

tight reach wind just forward of the beam.

on the wind 30° from the wind direction.

luffing to bring the boat's head into the wind (the sail would collapse).

running to sail directly downwind with the sails eased right out.

boom the spar attached to the bottom of the sail that pivots from the main mast.

leeward to face away from the direction the wind is coming from.

windward the direction from which the wind blows.

I have used a clock face to explain what point of sailing you are on. It's the same on both sides of the yacht; where the wind hits the yacht is that particular point of sailing.

The nearest angle you can sail to the wind is five-to or five-past the hour, and the sails are all the way in. The further aft the wind hits the boat, the further out the sails go.

Both sails are either all the way in or all the way out, or if the wind hits the boat on the beam, which is halfway, both sails are halfway out. All the way in is when you can't get the sails any further in.

The position of the main boom is also on the diagram.

Some
start line
terminology

Dial up   A manoeuvre by the starboard boat at the start to force the port boat to the least favoured end of the start area.

First cross   If the yachts have gone off on **split tacks** (different directions) at the start, the **first cross** is the first time the two yachts meet on opposite tacks. The yacht in first place crosses in front of the other yacht.

Layline   A **layline** is the best course the yacht is able to sail in order to get to the next mark without tacking or gybing.

Leverage   Teams constantly aim for more **leverage** or advantage against the opponent by using windshifts, knowing the most favoured end of the course, and sailing strategies.

Penalties   The umpires give a penalty to the yacht infringing the rules. The penalty is usually a 360° turn. If the red penalty flag is flown the penalty turn must be completed as soon as possible. At other times the yachts can complete a penalty turn when they choose.

If both yachts incur a penalty the penalties cancel each other out. Yachts have no rights on a penalty turn and will try to come out on starboard tack.

Pin   The start line is indicated with a committee boat at one end and a buoy at the other. The buoy is known as the **pin**.

Split tacks   At the start line the yachts may go across the line on the same tack but then split off so one yacht is on starboard tack and one yacht is on port tack. This is a split tack.

Time on distance   The **time on distance** is the time a yacht has to go until the start or from where they are to the next mark.

Transit lines   Transit lines are used by tacticians and skippers to assess the best layline for approaching the start line.

The start

The start sequence is possibly the most exciting part of the race and can have a huge impact on the rest of the race. Before the race there is a draw to decide which boat will approach the start line from the starboard end and which will approach from the port end of the line. The winner is able to decide their approach and this then alternates throughout the rest of the races between those two teams. This is known as alternating ends. The starboard approach boat flies a yellow flag from the **backstay** and the port-hand boat flies a blue flag.

Flags

The racing teams, race officials and umpires use several flags.

Blue flag   *(plain blue flag)*
Flown by the team approaching the start line from the port side.
If it is held up by the umpire this team has incurred a penalty.

Yellow flag   *(plain yellow flag)*
Flown by the team approaching the start line from the starboard end of
the line. If it is held up by the umpire this team has incurred a penalty.

*1. DELAYED PENALTIES   Unless a Red flag is displayed, a penalty may
   be undertaken at any time during the race.

*2. OFFSET PENALTIES   If both yachts have a penalty they cancel each
   other out, unless a Red flag is displayed.

Red flag   *(plain red flag)*
This is displayed with a blue or yellow flag and indicates that a team
has to do a penalty turn immediately.

Green flag   *(green flag with white diagonal stripe)*
Used by an umpire to indicate that no penalty is imposed.

Y flag   *(yellow and red diagonal stripes)*
This is the protest flag displayed by a team to indicate to the umpires
that they are protesting. The umpires then respond with the appropriate
flag indicating their decision.

Black flag   *(plain black flag)*
Held up to show that a team has incurred three penalties and is
disqualified. The other team wins.

The start sequence

The Race Committee Boat, which is at one end of the start line, uses flags and a gun signal to time the start. The following start sequence is used:

1. Attention signal: 11 minutes to the start

Gun plus D flag

(D flag is yellow with a blue stripe in the middle)

2. Warning signal: 10 minutes to the start

Gun plus F flag (replaces D flag)

(F flag is white with a red diamond shape at its centre)

3. Warning signal: 6 minutes to the start

F flag drops

4. Preparatory signal: 5 minutes to the start

Gun plus P flag. Yachts enter the course from their respective sides of the start line and engage in the prestart duel.

(P flag is blue with a white square in the middle)

5. Start

Gun plus P flag drops

The rules require that the yachts have to enter the start area within one minute of the gun and must enter from opposite ends of the start area. The boat that enters from the starboard side generally has the favoured end because it enters the area with the right of way. It is able to control what the other boat does and may do the dial-up manoeuvre by heading straight for the port tack boat, forcing it to tack away from the line. It is able to continue controlling the other boat and force it to the least favoured end of the line.

The most favoured end of the line depends on the wind strength and direction and is decided on by the tactician and the skipper before entering the start area. This can mean that the first boat across the line may not necessarily have the best start. The other boat might be behind but upwind of the first boat and so be in the best position to use windshifts.

The 'winner' of the start is usually the boat that heads across the other on the first cross on the **beat** upwind. If the yachts go off on split tacks they may not cross until they are a long way up the first leg.

The port boat may engage in **circling** as a defence and lead the starboard boat around the committee boat because the following boat is not able to go between it and the mark.

At the same time the skippers must be aware of their time on distance so that they always know how far they are away from the start, even if they are engaged in a duel with the other yacht to get to the favoured end of the line.

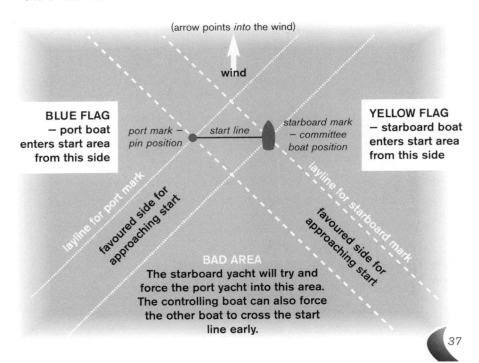

(arrow points *into* the wind)

wind

BLUE FLAG
– port boat
enters start area
from this side

port mark –
pin position

start line

starboard mark
– committee
boat position

YELLOW FLAG
– starboard boat
enters start area
from this side

layline for port mark

favoured side for approaching start

layline for starboard mark

favoured side for approaching start

BAD AREA
The starboard yacht will try and
force the port yacht into this area.
The controlling boat can also force
the other boat to cross the start
line early.

The upwind leg

As mentioned, the strength and direction of the wind is the key to always knowing the favoured side of the course or staying between the other competitor and the next mark, also forcing them to the less-favoured side of the course. Match-racing strategy focuses on predicting wind changes (both direction of and strength) and on staying in the favoured position. However, predicting and picking windshifts is not easy and even at this level of racing involves a bit of luck.

The **upwind leg** means that the yachts have to tack (zigzag) up to the mark, which is set by the race committee to be directly upwind from the start.

The yacht that has the advantage will be looking to see how it can **cover** the other yacht to avoid it getting to the favoured side of the course and then get ahead of it. The trailing yacht may try to tack clear of the other yacht but then the covering boat will tack on top of it. This kind of manoeuvring may continue right up to the top mark.

The tactician/strategist is constantly assessing the correct layline to approach the mark. The layline is the line the yacht can sail at maximum power straight to the mark without tacking. If the wind shifts the layline shifts.

Approaching the top mark is a critical time. There are rules for going around marks. Firstly, the buoys are always approached to starboard so that the yachts go round them in a clockwise direction. Secondly, there is the 'two boat-length circle' rule. This is an imaginary line two boat-lengths from the mark. The normal starboard tack right of way rule does not apply, as the outside boat must give room to the inside yacht whatever tack it is on.

The downwind leg

During the **downwind leg** the wind is behind the yacht. It can be a very important leg for the trailing yacht, which can block the wind of the boat ahead of it and may control the lead yacht's course and position.

Going downwind, the boats can almost never sail directly towards the next mark. The lighter the wind, the greater the angle at which the boat has to sail. This is done to keep speed up. Although the yachts may be able to sail straight to the mark, the fastest time to the mark is *not* necessarily via a straight line.

Choosing the correct sails and course is critical. If the wind is strong a spinnaker may be set, or in lighter winds the gennaker. Both sails are huge and gybing requires skilled sail-handling from the crew.

After going around the mark the yacht will do either a **bear away set** (meaning the crew set the spinnaker or gennaker as they go around the mark) or do a **gybe set** (meaning they set the spinnaker after they have **gybe**d). The latter is slower because the boat loses speed as it gybes.

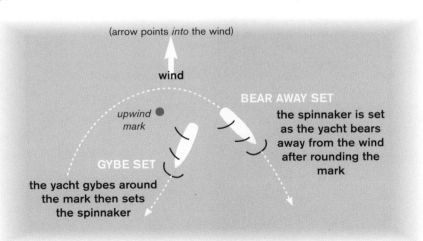

(arrow points *into* the wind)

wind

upwind
mark

BEAR AWAY SET
the spinnaker is set as the yacht bears away from the wind after rounding the mark

GYBE SET
the yacht gybes around the mark then sets the spinnaker

After deciding which tack to be on, the teams then 'tack downwind' because a boat goes faster with the wind on its side rather than right behind it. The team therefore has to decide if it will have the wind coming on the starboard side — and therefore have right of way — or if it will have the wind on the port side and have inside rights as it goes round the mark at the end of the leg.

Approaching the mark the yachts again have to adhere to the two-boat-length rule. Being between the other yacht and the mark is the favoured position because the rules state that a yacht must be allowed room around the mark. The outside boat has to give way and may be forced to sail a wider, longer course around the mark.

The last leg of the race is always a downwind run.

The *yachts*

All yachts that have raced in the Louis Vuitton and America's Cup since 1988 are in a specific class known as the International America's Cup Class (IACC). These boats must conform to the IACC rules. These rules have evolved due to controversy surrounding the interpretation of previous rules and because of races being held between extremely different boats. The first IACC yachts (now called ACC yachts) raced in 1991 in San Diego.

> The design parameters of the rules mean that while each boat is not identical, they are capable of similar performance. The aim is to have different boats racing on equal terms.

Formula

There is a specific formula that allows different yachts to race competitively. The formula sets out certain measurements for length, sail area and **displacement**, and must be adhered to. All yachts are inspected by the Technical Director during construction and before and during racing. A team outside the formula can be disqualified.

For the 2003 America's Cup, yacht designers will take into consideration the requirements of the skipper and the crew, and the changeable waters of the Hauraki Gulf.

The hull

The current boats are **monohull**s (one hull). They are constructed out of layers of carbon fibres and 'baked' to be very strong but light.

They have a number of appendages — **fins**, rudders, **bulb**s and wings. Fittings below the water contribute to drag so they have to be considered carefully. The design of the **keel** has become very important and there is a special day for each syndicate to reveal its keel.

The sails

The sails usually carried on board for a race day are one mainsail, five genoas, three gennakers and two spinnakers. However, these numbers will vary according to wind speed on the day.

Each yacht receives a consecutive class number that is displayed on its sail with the silhouette of the America's Cup above (this silhouette is the class insignia). Between 1990 and 2000, 62 America's Cup Class boats had been built. It is expected that about 19 new boats will be built before 2003. The new boats will race with numbers from 62 onwards. These numbers stay the same, even if the boat changes ownership.

Positions around the boat

1. aft   at or near the stern.
2. beam   the widest part of the boat.
3. forward   forward section of the boat.
4. bow   the front end of the boat.
5. port   the left side of the boat when looking forward.
6. starboard   the right side of the boat when looking forward.
7. stern   the rear end of the boat.

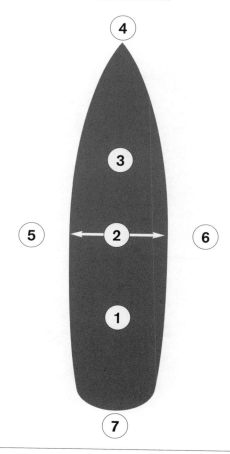

Parts of the boat

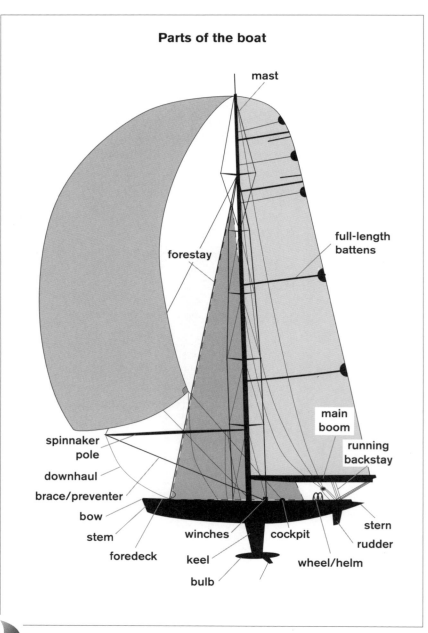

mast

full-length
battens

forestay

spinnaker
pole

main
boom

downhaul

running
backstay

brace/preventer

bow

stern

stem

winches

cockpit

rudder

foredeck

keel

wheel/helm

bulb

Sails

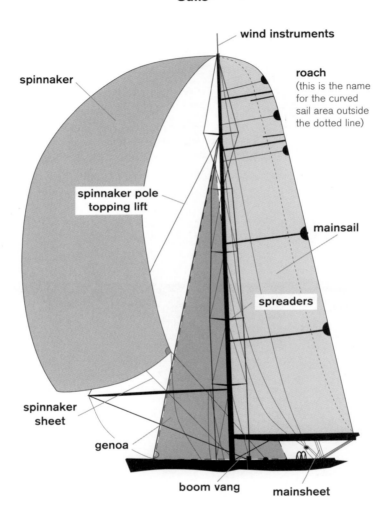

wind instruments

spinnaker

roach
(this is the name
for the curved
sail area outside
the dotted line)

spinnaker pole
topping lift

mainsail

spreaders

spinnaker
sheet

genoa

boom vang   mainsheet

*Note: The genoa and the spinnaker
are rarely up at the same time.*

Boat measurements

1. length overall (loa)   a boat's extreme length, measured from the foremost part of the bow to the aftermost part of the stern.

2. waterline length (wl)   the length of a boat at the waterline from stem to stern.

3. wetted surface   the area of the hull under water.

4. draft   the depth of water a boat requires in order to float. This is the vertical distance from the waterline to the bottom of the keel.

5. topsides/freeboard   the height of the side of the boat from the waterline to the deck.

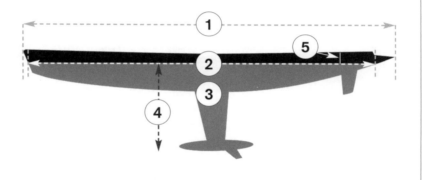

The *crew*

Each yacht is required to have 16 crew members.

A crew trains for years in preparation for the final regatta. Although each person has a clear role, the emphasis is on teamwork. Each crew member is required to be a good sailor who is strong, very fit and committed.

There can be one other person aboard who must not participate in any aspect of the race or sailing. This person usually sits behind the afterguard, at the back end of the yacht, and is sometimes referred to as the 17th man or the owner's representative or guest.

Crew positions

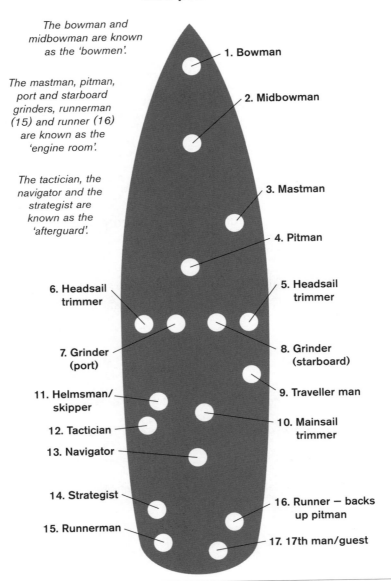

The bowman and midbowman are known as the 'bowmen'.

The mastman, pitman, port and starboard grinders, runnerman (15) and runner (16) are known as the 'engine room'.

The tactician, the navigator and the strategist are known as the 'afterguard'.

1. Bowman
2. Midbowman
3. Mastman
4. Pitman
5. Headsail trimmer
6. Headsail trimmer
7. Grinder (port)
8. Grinder (starboard)
9. Traveller man
10. Mainsail trimmer
11. Helmsman/ skipper
12. Tactician
13. Navigator
14. Strategist
15. Runnerman
16. Runner – backs up pitman
17. 17th man/guest

1. Bowman

The bowman can be involved in a number of roles. In a prestart manoeuvre he may be up on the bow calling time and distance to the starting line and conveying other important information about the start line and the opponent back to the helmsman. He attaches **halyard**s to hoist sails and **sheet**s to control the sails. Often in prestart he will help control the jib by **backing** it against the wind to stall the yacht. He organises the **foredeck** for the next sail hoist.

2. Midbowman

The midbowman works with the bowman. When the sails are lowered, he pulls them down into the hatch and packs them away. The midbowman is in charge of the storage of the sails below deck.

3. Mastman

The mastman is the big guy who helps the bowman and the midbowman. He leaps in the air and grabs the halyard (this action is called 'bouncing') to pull up the new sail at mark roundings or sail changes with the halyard at the mast, before the halyard goes to the grinders to be fully hoisted. He is also responsible for attaching the spinnaker pole to the mast as well as helping to gybe and to store the spinnaker pole. He is also involved in trimming and grinding the mainsail.

4. Pitman

The pitman calls the halyard tension. When the sail is completely hoisted, he works in conjunction with the foredeck crew. He also pulls the halyards that are being pulled by the mastman, controls ropes in the **cockpit** for the bowman and is the communication link to the crew that run the front of the yacht. He eases halyards for the dropping of the sails.

49

5 and 6. Trimmers

The correct trim of sails is one of the most vital aspects of a fast boat. A trimmer needs to be fit and strong and will have years of match-racing experience. There are two trimming positions for travelling upwind and downwind. Trimming the sails has everything to do with ensuring the correct sail shape, as good sail shape provides maximum power and boat speed. Experienced sailmakers sometimes make the best trimmers as they understand the shapes of the sails.

The trimmers of the **headsails** (the genoas and the spinnakers) work closely with the mainsail trimmer and the helmsman. Headsail trim is important for the balance and manoeuvrability of the yacht. Their trimming functions change according to whether the yacht sails upwind or downwind.

A spinnaker is used only on the downwind runs of the course for speed. It is a large billowing sail that requires careful trimming. The aim is to keep the large sail full so the trimmer is constantly letting the sail out and bringing it in. The trimmer calls the sail and the grinders work the **winches** to control the sheets that bring the sails in again.

7 and 8. Grinders (two people)

This group is also called the 'engine room'. The grinders respond to instructions to winch in the sail. They bring the sail in by grinding in on huge manual winches called coffee grinders (the yachts are not allowed electric winches). Grinders also hoist the mainsail and genoas using the grinders. There can be up to eight people grinding at one time. Without grinders the yacht is powerless.

9. Traveller man

When sailing downwind, a traveller trimmer will become a mainsail grinder. The mainsheet traveller is a metal track running across the yacht in front of the steering position. The track transfers the load of the sail from the sail to the helm of the yacht and is important for control of the yacht.

The traveller and mainsail trimmer work closely together to determine the correct mainsail shape and position.

10. Mainsail trimmer

Because the mainsail is so big — measuring between 200 and 225 square metres — it contributes significantly to the yacht's performance.

The mainsail trimmer works closely with the helmsman, the headsail trimmers and the strategist to ensure the correct trim of the mainsail is allowing the yacht maximum speed.

11. Helmsman (or skipper)

The helmsman is responsible for the boat and making the ultimate decisions after receiving information and advice on how the boat is sailing from the navigator, the tactician and the sail trimmers. The afterguard (the navigator and tactician) and the helmsman call **tactics** in the prestart positioning and in situations where they and the other boat are in close quarters.

12 and 14. Tactician and strategist

The strategist and tactician are key members of the crew. The tactician concentrates on the tactical position of the boat in relation to the position of its competition, and plans where his own boat wants to be on the race track. He relays this important information to the helmsman and the navigator.

The strategist knows the overall plan; he communicates with the on-the-water weather team before the race and also assists the tactician. The strategist is always looking up the course for any changes in conditions.

The tactician and the strategist have an intimate knowledge of race rules and they carefully consider sea, wind and tide change conditions.

13. Navigator

The navigator uses information from computers and instruments to make sure that the boat is on course, sailing the best course and speed for the start, rounding the marks and crossing the finish line. The navigator communicates with the helmsman, the tactician and the sail trimmers about time on distance, times to marks, laylines and general information regarding wind patterns.

15. Runnerman

The wires that tighten the backstays are called the runners. They run from the stern of the boat to the top of the mast on the windward side of the yacht. The tension of the backstays is crucial to the performance of the boat and for making sure the mast stays in the yacht.

The runner is let go when the yacht tacks from one side of the wind to the other. This has to be done quickly and smoothly so as not to jerk the top of the mast. The windward runner has to be winched tight during this manoeuvre.

16. Runner/pitman

This person works with the runnerman on upwind runs. He then moves forward on the boat to assist the pitman when rounding the marks.

The
course

In 2003, the Louis Vuitton Cup and the America's Cup
will be raced in the Hauraki Gulf, which is off the
East Coast Bays of Auckland, New Zealand.

The races in the Challengers Series are held in three areas, as shown in the
diagram on the next page. Which area is used is decided by wind
conditions on the day. In the following diagram, the three small circles
indicate the areas in which the races for the Louis Vuitton Cup will be
held. The races take place within an area that is bordered by the
Whangaparaoa Peninsula to the north, the mainland shore area of
Auckland to the west and Rangitoto Island to the south. Further east lie
Great Barrier Island and the Coromandel Peninsula.

On race day, two of these areas may be used to stage races, with the
other being used as a practice area by the Defender.

The large circle is the area that is used for the America's Cup races.

Race areas in the Hauraki Gulf

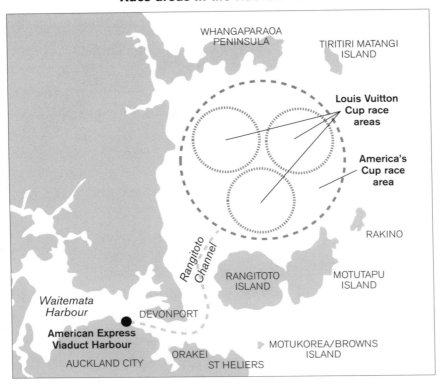

Race length

There are six legs in each race, as shown in the diagram opposite.

> The first and last legs, when the yachts cross the
> start/finish line, are 3.25 nautical miles long.
> The other four legs are 3 nautical miles long.
> This gives a total race length of 18.5 nautical miles,
> or over 34 kilometres.
>
> *(1 nautical mile is about 1.85 kilometres.)*

The course layout

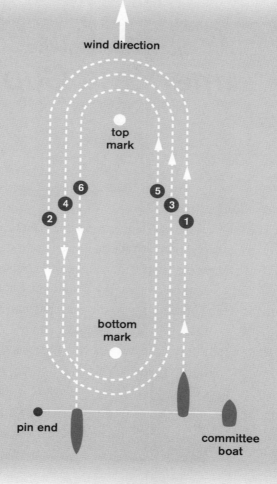

(arrow points *into* the wind)

wind direction

top mark

6 4 2 5 3 1

bottom mark

pin end

committee boat

A short history of the
America's Cup

The first challenge

During the late 1840s, American John Cox Stephens and five friends built a **schooner** that was very different from traditional yacht design at the time. They issued a race challenge to the Royal Yacht Squadron in England.

The Royal Yacht Squadron ran the race around the Isle of Wight, which was its island base. The prize for the winner was 100 guineas and a silver trophy.

On 22 August 1851, the yacht *America* won the race with a large lead. In 1857 a member of the 1851 winning syndicate gave the 'America's Cup' to the New York Yacht Club with the original Deed of Gift, thus establishing the idea of an international regatta between yacht clubs.

America versus England

Since the first challenge in 1869, the Cup has been a fiercely contested trophy. There have been regular challengers, about every three or four years, with large gaps around the time of the two world wars. The New York Yacht Club remained the Defender of the cup for 113 years.

Until the 1980s, competition was primarily between England and America, but England has never been successful.

One explanation has been the different approach each nation took towards the race. England's approach involved a belief in sport as the pursuit of amateurs with **Corinthian** yachting ethics and sportsmanship. This contrasted with the hard-nosed, professional ethics the Americans employed in all aspects of the defence, utilising the best designers and sailors in an all-out pursuit of victory.

Bigger and bigger

From the first challenge in 1869, until the Second World War, the yachts became progressively bigger. In order to be as fast as possible, the boats had a long **waterline length (wl)**, one mast, and they were gaff-rigged (meaning they had a four-sided mainsail) with a **topsail** above that. The ultimate long boat with huge rigs was *Reliance,* the Defender in 1903.

Designed by Nathanael Herreshoff, *Reliance* had a length overall of nearly 144 feet (40 metres). Her mast towered at 196 feet (60 metres) with over 16,000 square feet (1500 square metres) of sail. Herreshoff's innovative approach included two steering wheels, a hollow rudder that could be filled with water or pumped hollow for easier steering, winches with gears and ball bearings, lightweight steel **spar**s and a **topmast** that could be lowered into the **mainmast** if it wasn't being used.

Reliance raced against the Challenger *Shamrock III.* This was Sir Thomas Lipton's third America's Cup challenge. Lipton challenged the Cup five times but had no success.

The next regatta was in 1930, the year the J-boat era began. J-boats were built to the J-class rule, which specified a waterline length between 75 and 87 feet and a single mast. The rig underwent a dramatic change from gaff (four-sided) to three-sided Bermudan sails. The Bermudan is still the standard sail on America's Cup boats as they perform well into the wind, are efficient as they have less rigging and they have a smaller sail area. The American Defender, *Enterprise,* won the regatta, which was Sir Thomas Lipton's last.

The 1930s saw some close, exciting racing. The yachts were huge and demanded competent skippers and crew. In 1934 England came the closest they ever had to winning the Cup. They went into the 1937 challenge determined to win.

Aware of the English effort to succeed, Harold Vanderbilt built *Ranger*. With a steel hull, *Ranger* was very powerful and very fast, and she is the most famous J-boat. She had the maximum allowable waterline length of 87 feet, and a 165-foot mast made of duralumin. *Ranger* made a clean sweep of the series against the Challenger, *Endeavour II*. Sadly, *Ranger* was broken up during the Second World War for steel and lead. Of the America's Cup J-boats, only *Shamrock III* and *Endeavour II* survive.

Smaller but better

The next America's Cup was in 1958. Taking into consideration the economic climate and the huge cost of the J-boats, the Royal Yacht Squadron was asked by the Americans to recommend a smaller, less expensive racing yacht. These boats were called by the misnomer '12-metres', even though they were the largest racing yachts of the time. The name 12-metre referred to the International Rule requiring that the dimensions of the boat's length, beam, sail area and **topsides/freeboard** added up to 12 metres. Compared to the J-boats they were tiny, as they had a 45-foot waterline length and 1900 square feet of sail. They were actually about 20 metres in length.

The 12-metre era (1958–87) carried on the tradition of important advances in boat building and design. Some of these advances are now common aspects of modern yachts, including the reverse **transom**, and bulb keels.

The first regattas of this era were raced without much fuss as America kept its grip on the trophy. This began to change with the arrival of teams from Australia.

New challengers

In 1970, for the first time, Challenger trials were held between France and Australia. It was a contentious regatta. There were several wrangles between the challengers and the defenders and a nasty collision in the final race between Challenger *Gretel II* and Defender *Intrepid*. The incident stirred Australian resolve to bring the Cup to the Southern Hemisphere.

After participating in four more regattas, Australia's victory in the 1983 regatta ended the New York Yacht Club's control over the America's Cup. *Australia II* will be most remembered for her winged keel and the subsequent controversy about how legal and within the 12-metre rule it was. Dennis Conner, the skipper of the Defender *Liberty*, was the first American skipper to lose the America's Cup in 132 years.

The Royal Perth Yacht Club was the first successful Challenger of the America's Cup and held the next regatta off their homeport of Fremantle in Western Australia in 1987. Conner's determination paid off and he won the regatta.

The race in 1989, held off the west coat of America by the San Diego Yacht Club, was the most controversial in a long history of controversial racing. Two years of acrimonious court battles between New Zealander Michael Fay's Big Boat challenge and Dennis Conner resulted in a mismatch between a large, heavy **sloop** and an ultra-light **catamaran**. It also resulted in officials agreeing to a new set of rules for future regattas that would prevent similar, costly disputes.

Lighter and faster

The modern era of the America's Cup had arrived. The new International America's Cup Class yachts were lighter and faster than the 12-metre boats. Syndicates were able to build two boats to conduct trials. An international jury was set up. On-the-water umpires keep the competition tight, out of jury rooms and away from protest panels. Women, virtually invisible for over 100 years, were included in sailing crews.

NZL 32 (*Black Magic*)

In 1995, Team New Zealand challenged and won the Cup in NZL 32. After a 37-1 record in the Louis Vuitton Cup, Team New Zealand won 5-0 in the America's Cup regatta, leading the final race by six minutes.

In 2000, Team New Zealand again won the America's Cup with a 5-0 record, beating the Italian yacht *Luna Rossa* in the Defender's Series. New Zealand is now the only country other than America to successfully defend the Cup.

Although it has changed from a one-race event with one challenger and several defenders, to a match-racing regatta between one defender and competing challengers, the America's Cup has lost none of its mystique or challenge. It continues to provide a focus for yachting design and technology and is one of the ultimate challenges for sailors around the world.

A beginner's
guide to sailing
terminology

aback   describes a sail that the wind has struck on its back or wrong side. This would be caused by a wind change or a course change.

abeam   at right angles to the middle of a boat.

aft   at or near the stern.

afterguard   (also called the 'brainstrust') the group comprising the helmsman and his advisers on race strategy, that is, the navigator and the tactician.

apparent wind   a combination of true wind speed and the boat speed when sailing upwind. Apparent wind speed will always be more than true wind speed.

astern   behind the boat; to go astern is to steer the boat in reverse.

back a sail   to force a sail against the wind (sometimes by physically leaning against the boom). This manoeuvre is used to make a boat stop or slow down.

backstay   wire from the top of the mast to the stern of the boat to hold the mast up.

ballast   heavy weight, usually iron or lead, which is placed low in the boat to provide stability.

bash   *see* **beat/bash**

batten   a flexible strip of fibreglass inserted horizontally into a batten pocket in the outside edge of the sail to give the sail shape and support. There would be no support of the roach on the mainsail without battens.

beam   the widest part of a boat.

bear away   to steer away from the wind.

bear away set   to set the spinnaker on the same tack when rounding the mark.

beat/bash   to sail on a zigzag course upwind.

bilge   the lower inside area of the hull.

boom   the spar to which the foot of a mainsail is attached.

boom vang   a system used to hold the boom down, particularly when a yacht is sailing downwind, so that the surface of the mainsail facing the wind is at a maximum.

bow   the front of the boat.

brace/preventer   line and tackle that limits the movement of the boom, usually for reasons of safety (so the boom doesn't knock a sailor overboard).

broach   to heel over so the rudder comes out of the water, limiting steerage.

broad reach   with the wind aft, any point of sailing between a beam reach and running.

bulb   the lump of lead at the bottom of the keel to stabilise the yacht.

catamaran   a sailing boat with two hulls.

Challenger   a team challenging the current Defender of the America's Cup.

circling   a tactic where two boats do 360° turns at the same time, chasing each other to gain the advantage.

clear air   wind that is not disturbed by an opponent.

clew   the after, lower corner of a sail at the junction of the foot and leech.

close quarters   sailing very close together.

close-hauled   the point of sailing closest to the wind (30°). The sails are all the way in.

cockpit   the area behind the mast where the crew work.

Corinthian   a nineteenth and early twentieth century term for an amateur yachtsman.

course   the direction in which a vessel is steered or is steering.

cover   where a leading boat is directly to windward of the other boat and it disturbs the airflow onto its opponent. The trailing boat is forced to tack in the opposite direction to escape the disturbed wind going up- or downwind.

Cunningham hole   crinkle just above the tack to flatten the sail. It changes the shape of the sail, moving the airflow forward.

current   flow of water caused by tide or wind movement of the sea.

dead run   running with the wind blowing behind it.

deck   the covering over the hull used to walk on.

Deed of Gift   the original set of rules (1871) for the America's Cup.

Defender   the team defending its possession of the America's Cup. In 2003 the Defender is Team New Zealand.

dial up   a manoeuvre by the starboard boat at the start to force the port boat to the least favoured end of the start area.

dipping/dip/duck   a sudden change of course to pass behind another boat.

displacement   the weight of seawater displaced by the submerged part of the boat and which is exactly equal to the boat's weight.

downhaul   a rope fitted to pull down the spinnaker boom.

downwind   sailing a course with the wind behind.

downwind leg   sailing away from the wind.

downwind mark   the mark at the bottom of the course.

draft   the depth of water a boat requires in order to float, being the vertical distance from the waterline to the bottom of the keel.

dummy tacks   *see* **false tacks**

eye of the wind   the direction from which the waves/wind are coming. The wind causing the wave direction is called a **true wind**.

false tacks   also called **dummy tacks**. A tactic to trick the other boat whereby a trailing boat performs only half a tack and then returns to its original course without going about.

fins   *see* **wings/fins**

first cross   if the boats have gone off on split tacks (different directions) at the start, the first cross is the first time that the two boats go past each other.

foot   the bottom edge of the sail between the tack and clew.

foredeck   the deck area forward of the mast.

forestay   the foremost stay, running from the masthead to the bow.

foretriangle   also called the **J measurement**. The triangle formed between the mast, forestay and the deck.

forward   forward section of boat.

freeboard   height of the side of the boat from the waterline to the deck.

gennaker   an asymmetric spinnaker used in lighter breezes when sailing downwind.

genoa   a large headsail, which overlaps the mast.

go about   to turn the boat through the eye of the wind to change tack.

gybe   to change tack by turning away from the wind; by turning the bow of the boat towards the main boom, the mainsail goes to the opposite side.

gybe set   to go around a mark, gybe, and then set a spinnaker or gennaker.

halyard   rope or wire used to hoist and lower sails.

head   top of the sail attached to the halyard.

head to wind   the bow of the boat headed directly into the true wind.

heading   the direction the boat is heading according to the compass.

headsails   the genoas and the jibs.

heel   the leaning over of the boat due to pressure of the wind on the sails.

helm   another word for the tiller or wheel of a boat that steers it.

hull   the main body of a boat.

hull speed   theoretical maximum speed of a boat relative to its overall length.

in irons   describes a boat stalled head-to-wind, usually while tacking and unable to bear off one way or the other.

J measurement   *see* **foretriangle**

keel   underwater appendage that gives the yacht stability and lift going to windward.

layline   an imaginary straight line tracing between the boat and a mark.

lee/leeward   the direction opposite to the way the wind is blowing.

leech   the after edge of the sail from head to clew.

leeway   the sideways drift of a boat off its course to leeward.

length overall (loa)   the boat's extreme length, measured from the foremost part of the bow to the aftermost part of the stern.

leverage   teams constantly aim for more leverage or advantage against the opponent by using windshifts, knowing the most favoured end of the course, and sailing strategies.

luff   the forward edge of a sail.

luff up   bring the boat into the wind.

luffing   when a sail collapses.

mainmast   the single vertical spar that the sails and a boom are attached to.

mainsail   the sail attached to the mast and the boom.

mainsheet   a rope that controls mainsail shape. It is attached to the main boom. This sheet pulls the mainsail in and lets it out.

mainsheet traveller   a fitting that slides sideways in a track and is used to alter the angle of the mainsail.

mark   a buoy in the water.

mast   a vertical spar that holds up a sail or sails.

mast step   the place at which the bottom of the mast is fitted in the hull.

midships   area around the middle of the boat.

monohull   boat with only one hull.

off the wind   sailing downwind.

on the wind   sailing upwind.

overlap   when the following boat's bow crosses the lead boat's stern.

penalty   the umpires give a penalty to a boat infringing the rules.

pin   the start line is indicated with a committee boat at one end and a buoy at the other. The buoy is known as the pin.

port   the left side of the boat when looking forward.

pressure   wind strength.

rail   edge of the deck where the crew sit and where the deck meets the hull.

reach   to sail with the wind roughly on the beam.

rig   sails, mast and stays.

right of way   the boat which is on the starboard tack or which is windward has the right of way.

roach   the curved portion of a sail extending past a straight line drawn between two corners.

round robin   a series of races within a race. In terms of the America's Cup, they are the races held within the Louis Vuitton Cup competition, which determines the Challenger for the Cup.

rudder   a flat appendage at the rear of the boat, in the water, to steer the boat.

running   to sail directly downwind with the sails eased out.

running rigging   all of the moving lines such as halyards and sheets used in the support and control of sails and booms.

sailset every time a boat tries to change course it will change its sailset or shape.

schooner a boat with two masts, the shortest mast forward.

sea room the room in which a boat can manoeuvre without danger of collision or going aground.

sheet a rope controlling the shape of a sail.

sidestay/shroud wires, usually in pairs, reaching from the mast to the sides of the boat to prevent the mast falling sideways.

slogging tacking upwind.

sloop a single-masted boat with a mainsail and one headsail.

spar a general term for mast, booms and poles.

spinnaker a large, light, balloon-shaped sail set in front of the bow when the boat is off the wind.

split tack at the start line the boats may go across the line on the same tack but then split off so one boat is on starboard tack and one boat is on port tack. This is a split tack. It can also occur during a race.

spreaders horizontal struts attached to the mast, which spread the shrouds out from the mast and improve their support of the mast.

starboard the right side of the boat when looking forward.

stem the timber at the bow of the boat between the deck and the waterline.

stern the rear end of the boat.

tack the lower forward corner of the sail.

tack to change the boat from one side of the wind to the other, by either gybing or going about.

tactics using boating rules, the sea and the wind to one's advantage.

telltails pieces of thread attached to strategic parts of the sails to indicate air flow and sail lift.

tender smaller boat used to take crew, sails and gear on and off the boat.

tight covering   where the lead boat matches the trailing boat tack for tack.

tight reach   the wind is just forward of the beam.

time on distance   the time a boat has to go until the start or from where it is to the next mark.

topmast   the very top of a spar that can be bent to flatten the mainsail.

topping lift   rope or wire used to adjust boom height.

topsides/freeboard   the sides of a boat between the waterline and the deck.

track   the course a boat has made on the water.

track slides   these attach the mainsail to the mast.

transit lines   transit lines are used by tacticians and skippers to assess the best layline for the start, to a mark or to another boat.

transom   the flat surface forming the stern of the boat.

trim   to adjust the angle of the sails by means of sheets, so that they are at their best shape and angle to the wind.

true wind   *see* **eye of the wind**

true wind speed   the wind speed from a stationary point on the water (as opposed to apparent wind speed).

upwind   towards the wind.

upwind leg   the leg of a course that heads to where the wind is coming from.

veer   the wind veers when it changes direction.

velocity made good (vmg)   the speed a boat is making relative to the direction of the wind. When sailing upwind the best vmg is between 50° and 30° and when sailing downwind the best vmg is between 135° and 170°.

wake   the disturbed water left behind a boat.

waterline length (wl)   the length of a boat from stem to stern at the waterline.

weather side   the side of a boat on which the wind is blowing.

wetted surface   the area of the hull and other appendages under water.

wheel   *see* **helm**

winches   large drums that are used to winch in and hoist sails.

windward   the direction from which the wind blows.

windward mark   the mark of the course set upwind from the start line.

wings/fins   attachments at the bottom of a keel used for stability, to create lift and to help steering.

Notes and signatures

Notes and signatures

Notes and signatures